SHARON The SHARK
By Barbara Bamford

Art by Oliver Popowski

Copyright © 2024 by Barbara Bamford.

All rights reserved. This book or any portion thereof may not be reproduced or used in any manner whatsoever without the express written permission of the publisher, except for the use of brief quotations in a book review.

Published in the United Kingdom by:

Coalville C.A.N. Community Publishing
Memorial Square,
Coalville,
Leicestershire,
England,
LE67 3TU

First Published in 2020
ISBN 978-1-9168960-3-1

https://coalvilleccp.uk

Sharon the Shark was an unpopular fish.
She didn't like people one little bit.
As lockdown approached, because covid was here,
her tenants were angry, they all lived in fear.

Money was short and jobs hard to find.
Rents for their homes, well they just got behind.
But with Sharon the Shark it fell on deaf ears.
She wanted payments "right now" and not in arrears.

An idea came to Sharon, she thought it was funny.
"This is a way I can get some more money."
"I'll double the rents and get it in quickly,
but first I must rest as I'm feeling quite sickly."

She started to cough, her temperature high.
"Oh crikey!" she thought, I think I might die.
It happened that Sunny was watching close by.
"What's up with you?" he said with a sigh.

"It's the same every year, you've got the flu,
count yourself lucky covid hasn't got you."
"Think of your tenants, they have little money,
and with covid around it's not so funny."

So she thought of Oli and her family of 8.
"It must be hard for her to put food on the plate,
she's a single mum, with no one to help.
How can she afford anything else on top of my rent?"

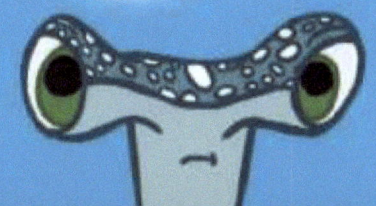

She thought of Curly who'd recently left home.
"How does he cope, the first time on his own.
He's young and ambitious, doing his best to live.
If he'd less bills to pay how much more could he give?"

She thought of Prickly who was trying to save,
to start a family with his friend Puffer Maeve.
They should be excited, but no they were scared,
because of the threat of rent hikes they had heard.

"If I put the rents down how nice would it be,
and the tenants, I'm sure will no doubt agree."
Do I need extra cash, I've enough, surely?
Could it be my greed that's making me poorly?"

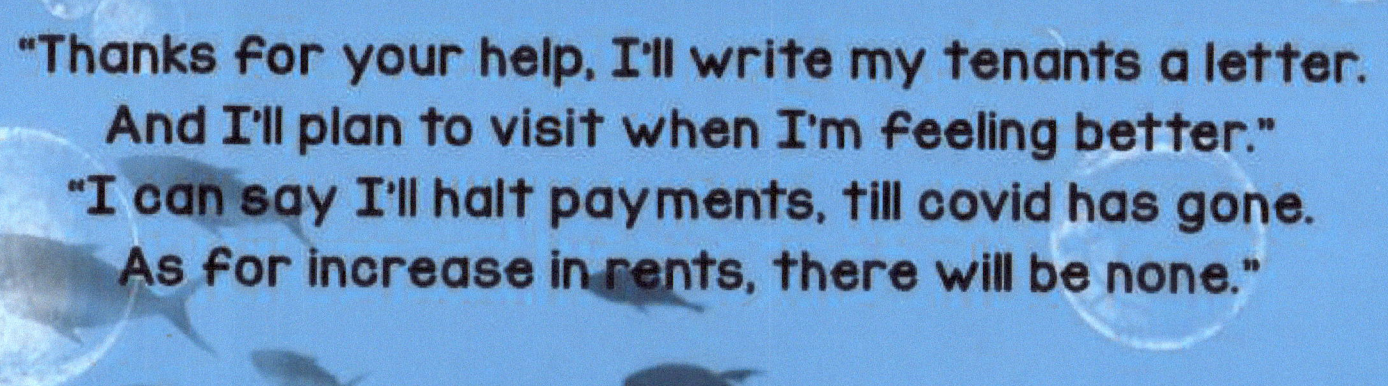

"Thanks for your help, I'll write my tenants a letter.
And I'll plan to visit when I'm feeling better."
"I can say I'll halt payments, till covid has gone.
As for increase in rents, there will be none."

All these good doings made Sharon Shark smile.
It was better than being greedy, bitter and vile.
"All I used to think about was making more money.
My world used to be dark. Now it is sunny."

Her tenants when they heard were so overjoyed.
It was nice to see Sharon when she wasn't annoyed.
She loved it so much, she decided to stay,
No 'absentee landlord' for Sharon from this day.

It was alright in the end.
Thinking of 'Other Peoples Views'.
We can all make a difference,
it depends what we choose.

Discover

O.P.V

plus more fun

Tool related activities

on our website

www.thinkfc.org.uk

O.P.V (Other peoples views)

A simple and fun Tool!

If you ever want help looking at the perspective of others.

1. **MAKE** a hat – It's simple.

2. **TH!NK** about who it represents.

3. **WRITE** or **DRAW** the names of the person/people on the hat.

4. **PRETEND** you are them by wearing it to **TH!NK** about the issues from the other persons perspective.

1. Take an A4 peice of paper.

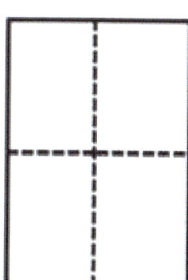

2. Fold in half – and in half again. Open out.

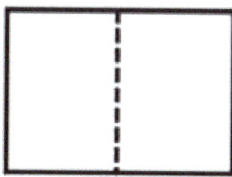

3. Fold in half along the short edge. Keep this edge at the top.

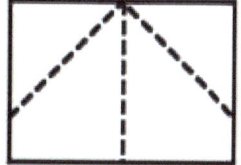 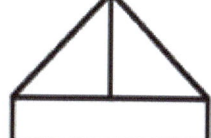

4. Fold the top two corners of the folded edge into the middle of the centre line.

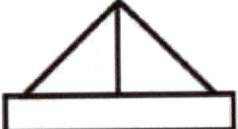

5. On each of the sides, fold the bottom-flaps up and over twice to make th rim of the hat.

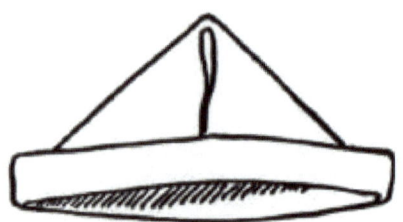

6. Use the hat for lots of things!

You can use it when you are on your own and want to see the perspectives of others.

Have a look at the prompts on the next page to help you decide HOW you might you involve others.

WHAT other situations might this possibly be used for?

WHO might you share this with?

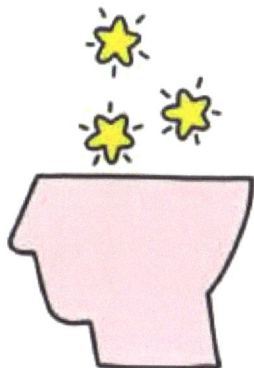
Is creative

Is good at it

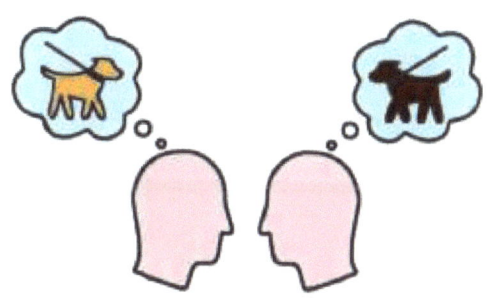
Has the same interests

It might be an opportunity

Has time

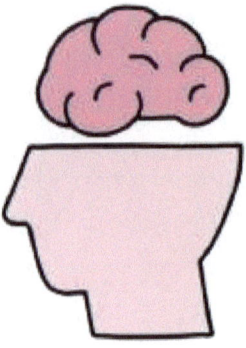

Has knowledge

Has connections

Has followers

 **Has the same values**	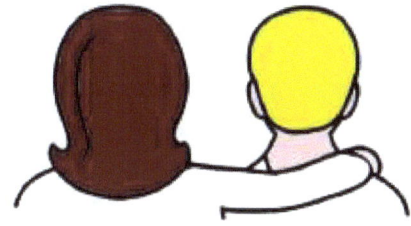 **Is a friend**
 **Will listen**	 **Is honest**

 **Has space**	 **Has experience**
 **Has money**	 **Has control**

 **Is family**	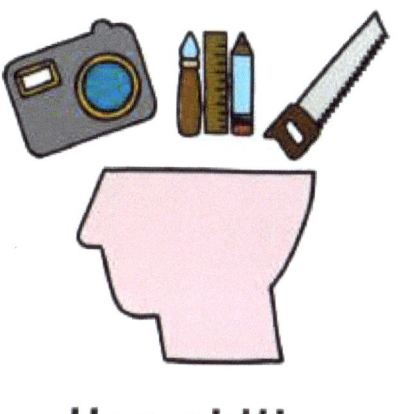 **Has skills**
 **It is their job**	 **Has ideas**

www.ingramcontent.com/pod-product-compliance
Lightning Source LLC
Chambersburg PA
CBHW040031050426
42453CB00002B/80